INSIDE MY BODY

MUSCLES

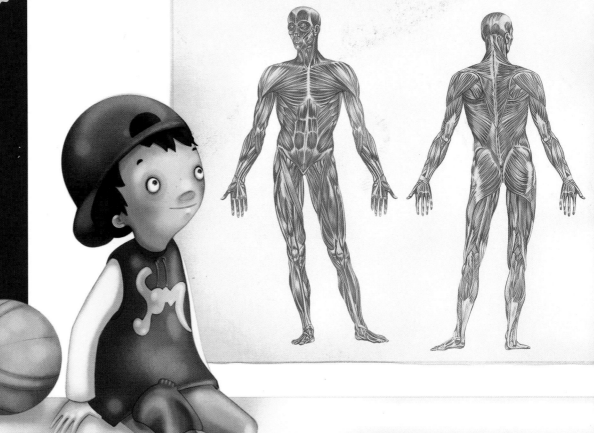

WRITTEN BY JUDY JENSEN SHAFFER ILLUSTRATED BY TERESA ALBERINI

amicus illustrated

Amicus Illustrated is published by Amicus
P.O. Box 1329, Mankato, MN 56002
www.amicuspublishing.us

Library of Congress Cataloging-in-Publication Data
Shaffer, Jody Jensen, author.
 My muscles / by Jody Jensen Shaffer ; Illustrated by
Teresa Alberini.
   pages cm. — (Inside my body) (Amicus illustrated)
 Summary: "A boy named Lucas has injured his calf
muscle at recess. Lucas and his classmate Mia discuss
the body's muscles"—Provided by publisher.
 Audience: K to grade 3.
 ISBN 978-1-60753-757-1 (library binding) —
ISBN 978-1-60753-856-1 (ebook)
 1. Muscles—Juvenile literature. 2. Musculoskeletal
system—Juvenile literature. 3. Human physiology—
Juvenile literature. I. Alberini, Teresa, illustrator.
II. Title.
 QP321.S463 2016
 612.7'4—dc23   2014041504

Editor: Rebecca Glaser
Designer: Kathleen Petelinsek

Printed in the United States of America at
Corporate Graphics in North Mankato, Minnesota.

10 9 8 7 6 5 4 3 2 1

ABOUT THE AUTHOR

Jody Jensen Shaffer is the author of 19
books of fiction and nonfiction for children.
She also writes poetry, stories, and articles
for children's magazines. When she is not
writing, Jody copy edits and proofreads
for children's publishers. She tries to keep
her body healthy by walking regularly and
eating nutritious foods. Visit Jody on the
web at jodyjensenshaffer.blogspot.com.

ABOUT THE ILLUSTRATOR

Teresa Alberini has always loved painting
and drawing. She attended the Academy
of Fine Arts in Florence, Italy, and she now
lives and works as an illustrator in a small
town on the Italian coast. Visit her on the
web at www.teresaalberini.com.

"Are you okay, Lucas?"

"I think I pulled a muscle, Mia. I need to go to the nurse's office."

"Which muscle is it?"

"The back of my lower leg—my calf muscle."

"Did you warm up before you played, Lucas?"

"No."

"Warming up before you exercise helps your muscles, remember?"

"Right, we learned that in health. And we have a health test today!"

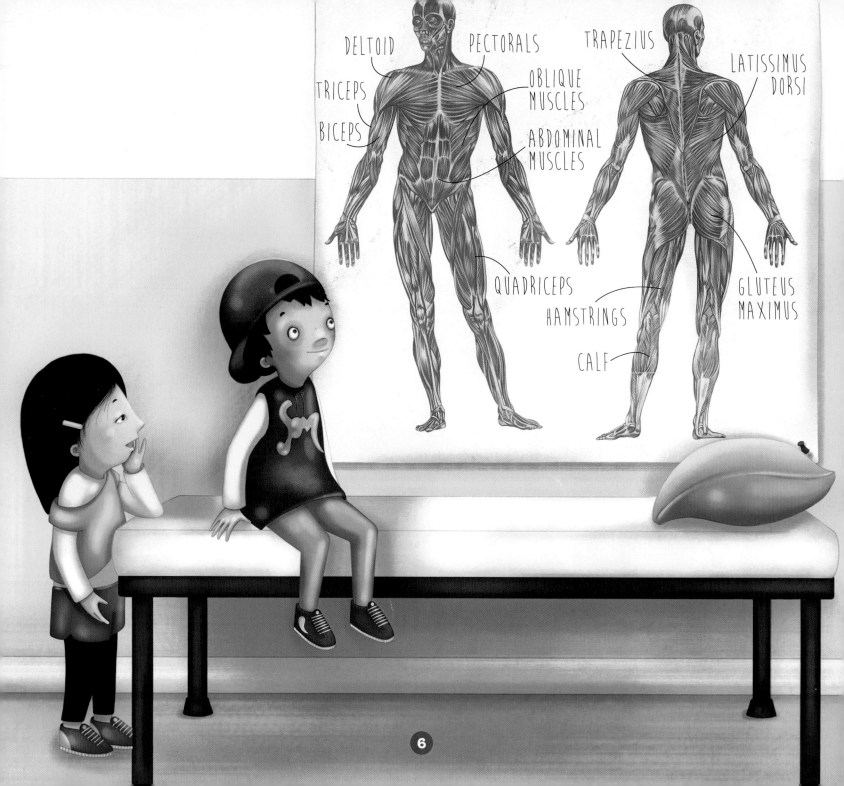

DELTOID

TRICEPS

BICEPS

PECTORALS

OBLIQUE MUSCLES

ABDOMINAL MUSCLES

TRAPEZIUS

LATISSIMUS DORSI

QUADRICEPS

HAMSTRINGS

CALF

GLUTEUS MAXIMUS

"I'll quiz you while we wait for the nurse. How many skeletal muscles do we have?"

"More than 600."

"And why are they called skeletal muscles?"

"Your muscles move your bones. Strong cords called tendons attach your muscles to your bones."

"My turn, Mia. How do your muscles work?"

"In pairs. When I kick a ball, the muscle in the front of my leg contracts, or gets shorter. My calf muscle relaxes, or gets longer."

"How do muscles know when to contract and relax?"

"Your brain tells them. When you decide to shoot a basket, your brain sends messages to your muscles. The signals travel through thin cords called nerves. Then your muscles know what to do."

CALF CONTRACTS   CALF RELAXES

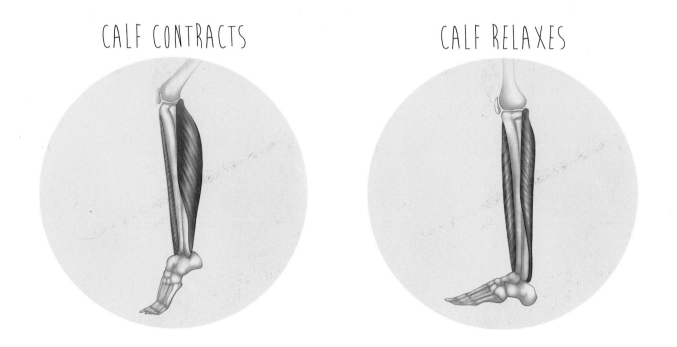

"Lucas, what happened?" said the nurse.

"I fell playing basketball at recess. Now I can barely walk."

"If your muscles stretch too far, it causes a strain."

"It really hurts."

"Put this ice pack on it. Rest and keep your leg up until class starts."

"Lucas, for our test, we need to know the other types of muscles."

"Yes. There's cardiac muscle in your heart. It pumps your blood through your body."

"And you don't have to think about it. Your brain sends messages to keep it pumping."

HEART MUSCLE

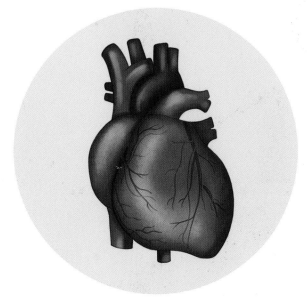

"After all this review, I bet we'll ace our health test! Remember the other kind of muscles?"

"I almost forgot about the smooth muscles. They push food through your stomach and blood through your blood vessels."

"And they make up all your organs."

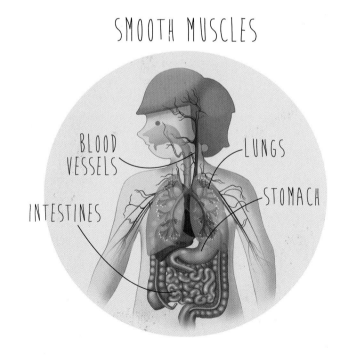

SMOOTH MUSCLES

BLOOD VESSELS

LUNGS

INTESTINES

STOMACH

17

"Time to go back to class, Lucas. Can you walk?"

"I can make it."

"Okay. Once we get there, follow nurse's orders and rest your calf. You need healthy muscles."

"I know, I know."

"And eating well is good for your muscles, too. Eat foods with protein, like meat and eggs. Exercise helps, too."

"What, are you the nurse now?"

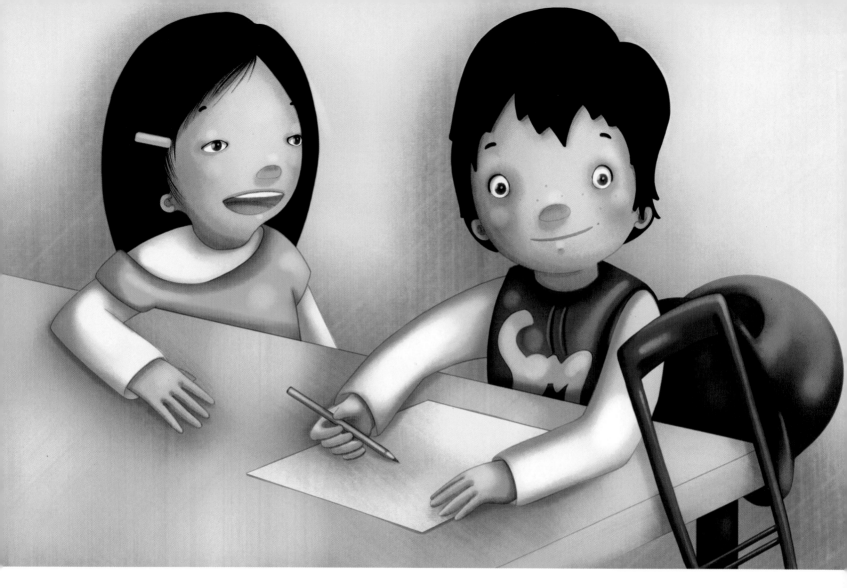

"Just looking out for you, Lucas."

"When my leg heals, let's play one-on-one."

"You're on! But next time, warm up first!"

BODY BY THE NUMBERS

Skeletal Muscles – More than 600

Biceps – 2

Calf – 2

Face – 42

Quadriceps – 2

Triceps – 2

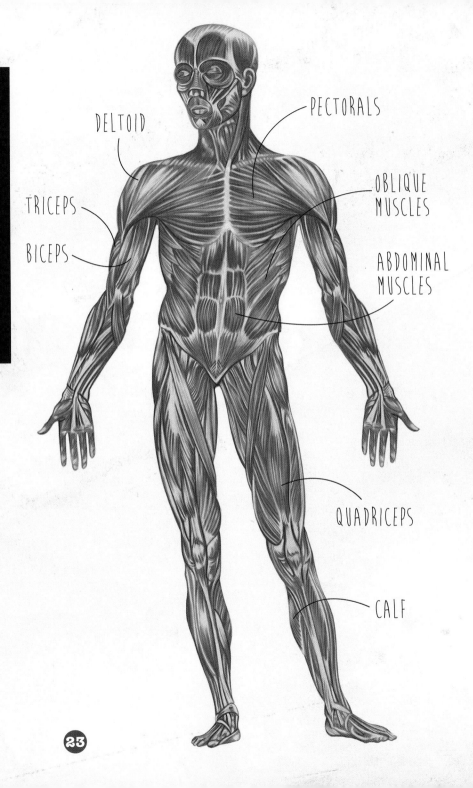

DELTOID

PECTORALS

TRICEPS

OBLIQUE MUSCLES

BICEPS

ABDOMINAL MUSCLES

QUADRICEPS

CALF

GLOSSARY

contract—To squeeze together and become shorter.

muscle—A group of body tissues that contract and move.

nerve—Fibers that carry messages from the brain to all parts of the body.

relax—To lengthen and become looser.

smooth muscle—The type of muscle found in your organs.

strain—An injury that happens when a muscle is hurt due to overuse or lack of warming up prior to exercise.

tendon—A strong cord that attaches your muscles to your bones.

READ MORE

Brett, Flora. **Your Muscular System Works!** North Mankato, Minn.: Capstone Press, 2015.

Gold, Susan Dudley. **Learning about the Musculoskeletal System and the Skin**. Berkeley Heights, NJ: Enslow Publishers, 2013.

Rose, Simon. **Muscular System**. New York: AV2 by Weigl, 2015.

WEBSITES

The Children's University of Manchester: The Muscles
www.childrensuniversity.manchester.ac.uk/interactives/science/exercise/muscles/
See an animated diagram of how muscles contract and relax.

Easy Science for Kids: Muscles – The Human Body
easyscienceforkids.com/all-about-human-body-muscles
Read about the muscles and watch a video explaining how they work.

KidsHealth: How the Body Works
kidshealth.org/kid/htbw/
View movies, do activities, and read more about how all parts of your body work.

Every effort has been made to ensure that these websites are appropriate for children. However, because of the nature of the Internet, it is impossible to guarantee that these sites will remain active indefinitely or that their contents will not be altered.